Animal Knock-Knock Jokes

Einstein Sisters

KidsWorld

Polar

KNOCK, KNOCK.

Who's there?

Alaska.

Alaska who?

Alaska one more time, will you please let me in?

Bear

The polar bear likes to **swim** in icy Arctic waters. It has a thick coat and a layer of **blubber** to keep it warm. The polar bear can close its nostrils when it swims **underwater**.

A polar bear's favourite food is ringed seals. It will also eat bearded seals, fish, ducks, geese, walruses and whales, when it can catch them.

Walrus

Clams are the walrus' favourite food. To find them, the walrus swims along the ocean floor and squirts water from its mouth, blasting the clams out of the sand.

The walrus uses its tusks to hold on to sea ice when it sleeps and to pull its body out of the water onto the ice.

Pika

The pika is
a small animal
that lives in the
Rocky Mountains.
It is about the same
weight as an orange.

KNOCK, KNOCK.

Who's there?
Pika.
Pika who?
Pika on
someone
your own size!

The pika collects fresh grasses, flowers and thistles in summer and lays them in the sun until they dry out like hay. Then it piles them into haystacks.

Giraffe

To drink from a watering hole, the giraffe has to **spread** its legs wide so its head can reach the ground.
A **giraffe's tongue** is black at the front and pink at the back. The front is black so it won't get **sunburned** when the giraffe is using it to pull **leaves** off trees.

Waxy Tree Frog

Anita who?

Anita another kiss, sweetie!

The waxy tree frog can't **jump**. It climbs through the trees holding the branches with its hands and feet.

Waxy tree frogs love to lay in the sun. The wax on the frog's skin keeps it from drying out or getting sunburned.

Gannet

The gannet's
main food is fish,
but it also eats squid.

It **plunge-dives** to catch its food.
It flies high over the ocean, and when it **spots
a fish,** it folds its wings against its body and
dives **headfirst** into the water. During
these dives, the bird can go up to
100 km/hour, about as fast
as a car drives on
the highway.

KNOCK, KNOCK.

Who's there?

Luke.

Luke who?

Luke out below!

Red Fox

The red fox
is the **most common**
type of fox in the world.
Not all red foxes have **red fur.**
They can be brown, black or silver.
The **tip of their tail** is
always white.

Verreaux's sifaka is a type of lemur. It lives in Madagascar. This sifaka spends most of its time in trees. It climbs in the branches or leaps from trunk to trunk.
To move around on the ground, it stands on its hind legs, holds out its arms and hops sideways.

Sifaka

Hippo

KNOCK, KNOCK.

Who's there?
Hippo.
Hippo who?
Hippo birthday to you!
Hippo birthday to you!

Male hippos spin their tails as they poo, **spraying** it in all directions to keep other male hippos away. Hippopotamuses can sleep **underwater.** They float up to take a breath. Then, still sleeping, they **sink** back down again.

Alpaca

Alpacas have a super soft coat, which is a lot like sheep's wool but not as itchy.

Alpacas have a nasty habit of spitting at each other when fighting for food.

A group of alpacas living together will use the same spot to go to the bathroom so they don't mess up their pen.

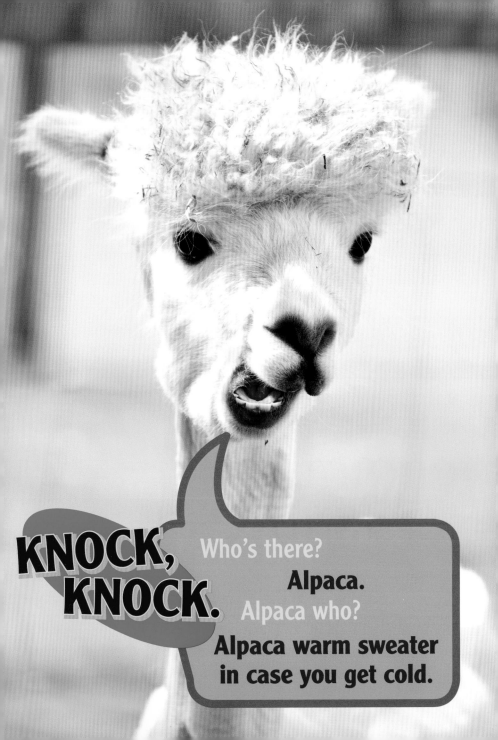

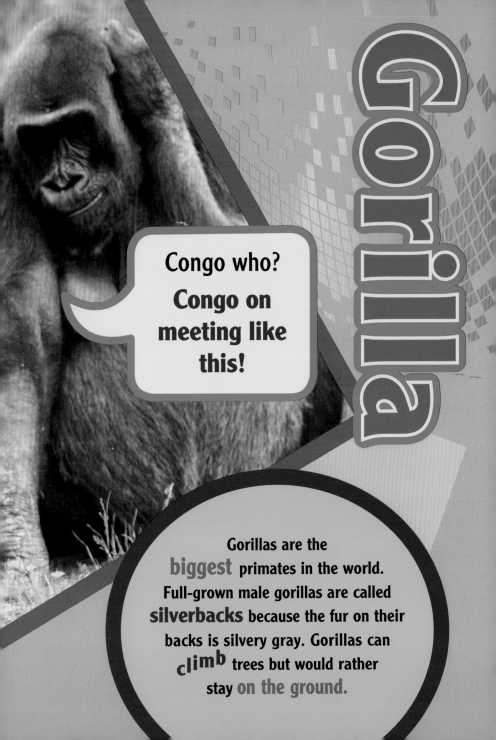

Orca

Orcas are
also called **killer
whales** even though they
are a **type of dolphin.** They
live in **large** family groups called **pods.**
Orcas "talk" to each other by making
different sounds, like
whistles and clicks.

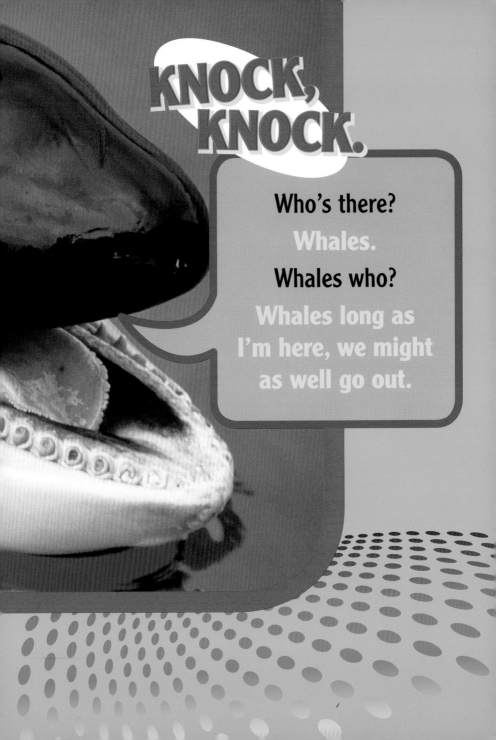

Ostrich

The ostrich is the **tallest** and **heaviest** bird in the world. The ostrich **cannot fly**, but it is a **great runner.** It can run faster than any other **2-legged** animal.

Zebra

KNOCK, KNOCK.

Who's there?
Kenya.
Kenya who?
Kenya get me a drink? I'm thirsty!

A zebra's stripes help keep it safe from predators like lions and hyenas. The wavy lines help it blend in with tall grass. When a group of zebras stands together, they look like a giant stripey mass to a lion, so it can't pick out a single zebra to attack.

Chipmunks have **four toes** on their front feet and **five toes** on their back feet! Chipmunks don't store fat when they **hibernate.** They store a lot of food to eat during winter.

Chipmunk

Great Horned Owl

The **great horned owl** is one of the only animals that eats **skunks.** It also eats mice, rabbits, bats, other birds and sometimes cats.

The great horned owl doesn't only say "hoo." It can also whistle, **scream,** bark, coo and **hiss.**

To protect its nest, this owl will **flap** its wings, clap its beak together and kick the unwanted guest with its feet. Its toes have sharp nails, called **talons,** that can tear skin.

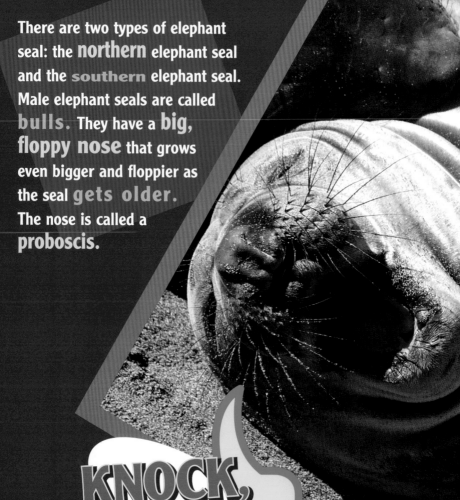

There are two types of elephant seal: the **northern** elephant seal and the southern elephant seal. Male elephant seals are called **bulls.** They have a **big, floppy nose** that grows even bigger and floppier as the seal gets older. The nose is called a **proboscis.**

KNOCK, KNOCK.

Who's there?

Danielle.

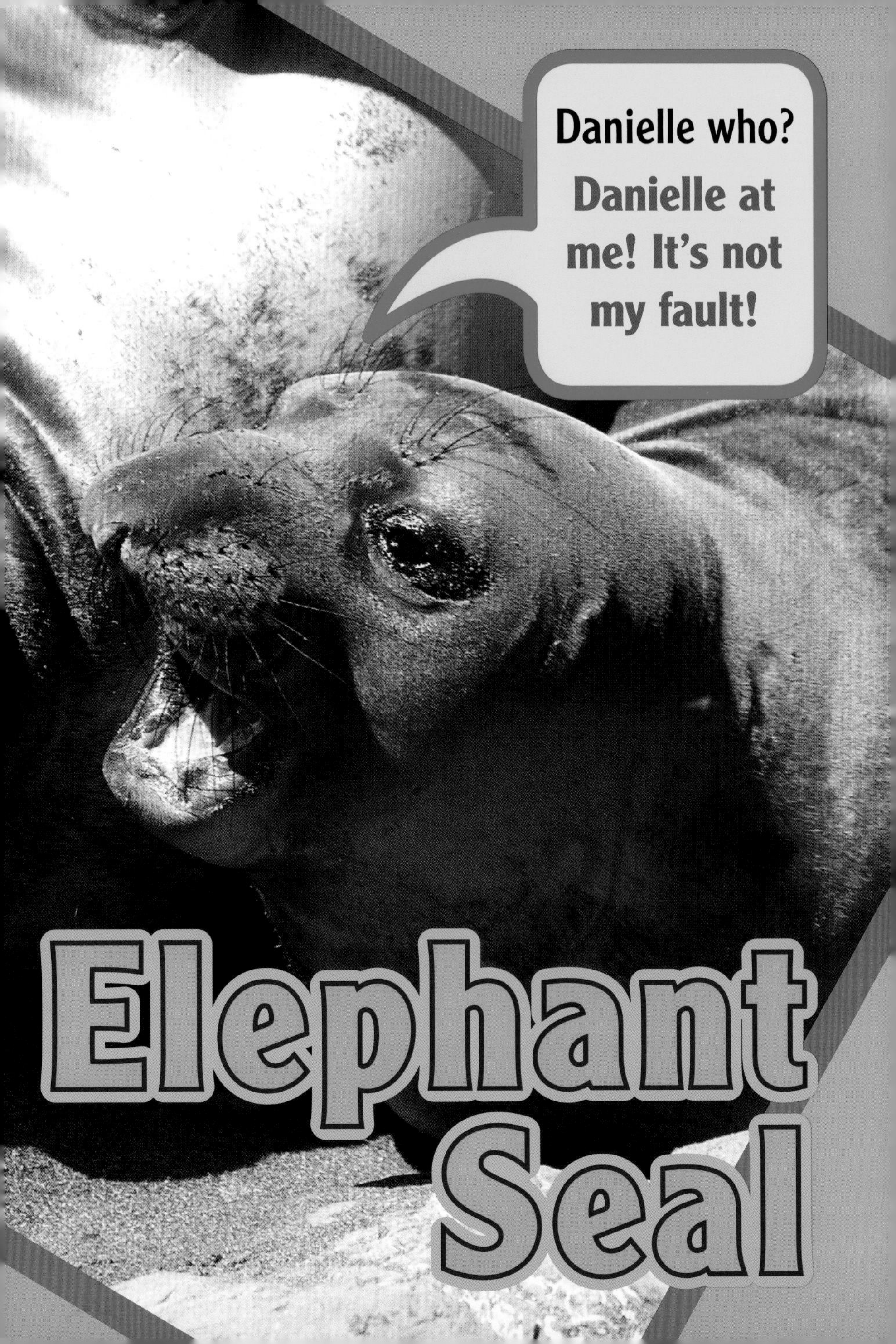
Danielle who? Danielle at me! It's not my fault!
Elephant Seal

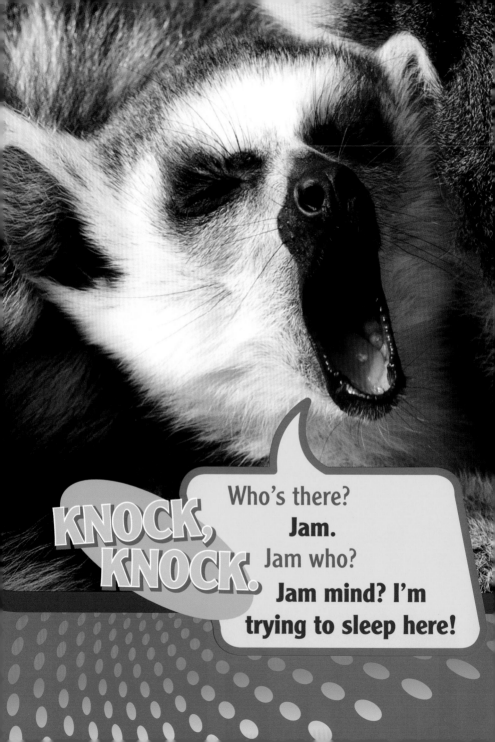

Lemur

Ring-tailed lemurs, like all lemurs, live in **Madagascar.**
They eat fruit, leaves, **flowers** and sap.
Most types of lemurs prefer to **stay in trees**, but ring-tails also spend a lot of time on the ground.

Muskox

Muskoxen live in the Arctic.
They are one of the only hoofed
animals that survived the last Ice Age.
Muskoxen have thick, shaggy fur to keep them
warm. Their coat has two types of fur. The
outer fur is called guard hair. It is almost
long enough to touch the ground. The
inner hair is called qiviut.
It is short, soft and woolly.

Who's there?
Wallaby.
Wallaby who?
Wallaby my friend?

Wallaby

A wallaby is a **smaller cousin** of the kangaroo. It lives in Australia. Wallabies are **marsupials.** They **carry their baby** in a **pouch** on their belly until the baby is old enough to protect itself.

KNOCK, KNOCK.

Who's there?

Howl.

Howl who?

Howl you know if you don't open the door?

Wolves live in packs. Each pack is made up of family members. Wolves **howl** to keep in touch with other members of **their pack**, and to warn other packs away from **their territory**.

Wolf

The wolf's sense of smell is about 100 times better than ours.

Gibbon

Gibbons spend most of their time in **trees.** To move around in trees, they swing by their arms from **branch to branch.** This is called **brachiation.** Gibbons can brachiate faster than any other monkey or ape.

Ibis

KNOCK,
KNOCK.

Who's there?
Ibis.
Ibis who?
Ibis seeing you!

The scarlet ibis is a **tropical bird.** It lives in swampy areas or **along shorelines.**
This bird eats a lot of shrimp and other red shellfish. The colour of the shellfish turns its feathers **red.** Young ibises have greyish feathers. As they get older, their feathers turn red.

Despite what
you see in cartoons,
a tortoise or turtle cannot
crawl out of its shell. The shell is
actually part of its rib cage and backbone.
Because the tortoise is attached
to its shell, it feels pain if the
shell gets cut or broken.

Tortoise

KNOCK, KNOCK.

Who's there?

Oslo.

Oslo who?

Oslo down!
What's the hurry?

KNOCK, KNOCK.

Who's there?
Ya.
Ya who?
Boy, you sure are excited to see me!

Grizzly Bear

Grizzly bears walk
on all fours, but **curious** bears
will stand on their **back legs** to get a
better look or smell. Some people think
that a bear on its hind legs is about
to **attack,** but that is
just a myth.

Gentoo Penguin

Gentoo penguins **swim faster** than any other type of diving bird. They build nests out of **pebbles and grass** for their eggs. Both parents help take care of the **chicks.**

Eel

Eels look like **water snakes,** but they are actually a type of fish.

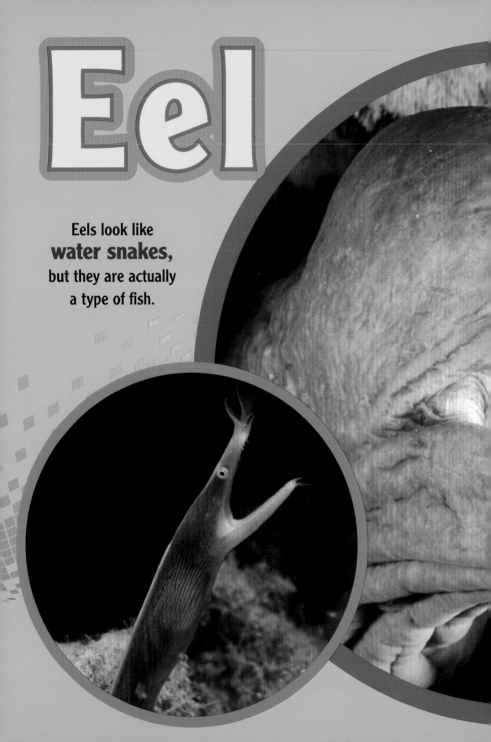

KNOCK, KNOCK.

Who's there?
Eel.
Eel who?
Eel be back!

Eels are one of
only a few types of
fish that can **swim
backward.** They can
even **move about on land**
for a few hours at a time.

Monkey

Monkeys are divided into two types: Old World monkeys and New World monkeys. Old World monkeys live in Africa and Asia. New World monkeys live in South America. The Barbary macaque from Africa is the only monkey that lives in the wild in Europe. It lives in Gibraltar.

Knock, knock.
Who's there?
Banana.
Banana who?

Knock, knock.
Who's there?
Banana.
Banana who?

Knock, knock.
Who's there?
Banana.
Banana who?

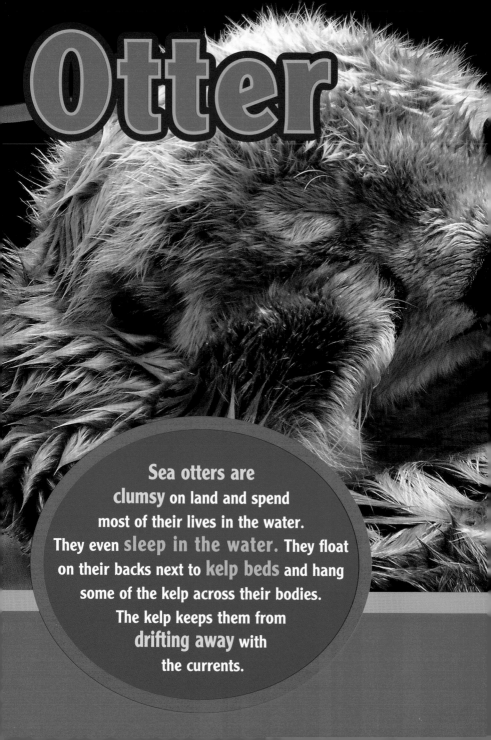

Otter

Sea otters are
clumsy on land and spend
most of their lives in the water.
They even sleep in the water. They float
on their backs next to kelp beds and hang
some of the kelp across their bodies.
The kelp keeps them from
drifting away with
the currents.

Alligator

The alligator has a round, almost **U-shaped snout**. It is usually **greyish**. When its mouth is closed, its bottom **teeth are hidden** by the upper jaw.

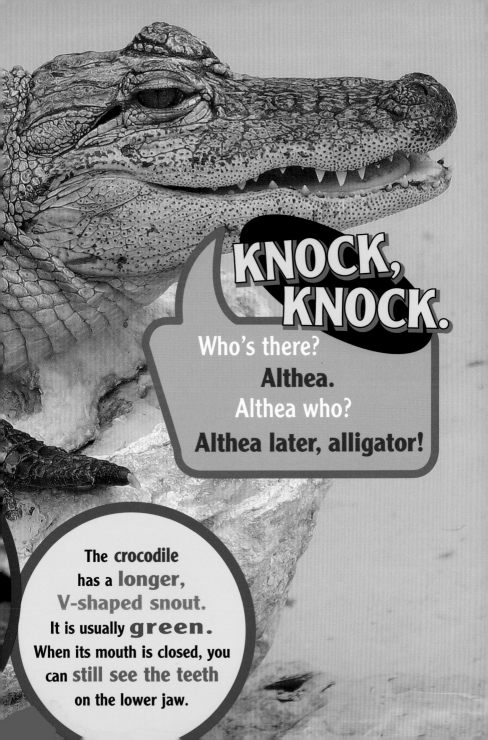

KNOCK, KNOCK.
Who's there?
Althea.
Althea who?
Althea later, alligator!

The crocodile
has a **longer**,
V-shaped snout.
It is usually **green.**
When its mouth is closed, you
can **still see the teeth**
on the lower jaw.

The Publisher: KidsWorld Books

Library and Archives Canada Cataloguing in Publication

Animal knock knock jokes / Einstein Sisters.

ISBN 978-0-9938401-7-3 (pbk.)

1. Animals—Juvenile humor. 2. Canadian wit and humor (English). I. Einstein Sisters, author

PN6231.A5A55 2014   jC818'.602   C2014-904199-3

Cover Images: Front cover: Cathy Keifer/Thinkstock. *Back cover:* zebra, Four Oaks/Thinkstock; gannet, Pi-Lens/Thinkstock.
Background Graphics: abstract swirl, hakkiarslan/Thinkstock, 3, 9, 15, 26, 30, 39, 51, 58, 62; abstract background, Maryna Borysevych/Thinkstock, 13, 25, 36, 49, 57, 61; pixels, Misko Kordic/Thinkstock, 4, 17, 20, 23, 28, 32, 43, 44, 52, 54.
Photo Credits: Thinkstock: Ben, 185, 56–57; Brandon Alms, 8; Cathy Keifer, 10–11; Christine Brassington, 60–61; David Thyberg, 17; DougLloyd, 6–7; Enjoylife2, 22–23; Four Oaks, 29; frostyy1108, 27; Fuse, 52, 62–63; garytog, 33; GatorDawg, 43; Hagforsen, 14–15; halbrindley, 5; Hemera Technologies, 38–39; Hugh Lansdown, 16; Humpata, 9; Ijdema, 36–37; Injo, 46–47; Irmantas Lukosiunas, 45; james63, 50–51; john henderson, 6; JohnCarnemolla, 26; Jupiterimages, 18–19, 32; Lori Skelton, 62–63; luckyraccoon, 59; Lynn_Bystrom, 42–43; manfredxy, 48–49; Marco Saracco, 40; matt-scherf, 41; Matthew Bassett, 58; mitchii, 53; Peter_Nile, 34–35; photohomepage, 2; Pi-Lens, 12–13; pigphoto, 44; pum-eva, 15; Purestock, 18, 54–55; robertdewit66, 54; robynleigh, 21; SamCastro, 46; ShinOkamoto, 20; Stephanie Delay, 4; TANZANIANIMAGES, 28; Tom Brakefield, 24–25; Tony Campbell, 51; UrsulaR, 30; Wayne97, 31.

We acknowledge the financial support of the Government of Canada.

Funded by the Government of Canada
Financé par le gouvernement du Canada | **Canadä**

PC: 37